Savings,

& investments

Written by **Niki Chesworth**

Illustrated by **Becky Cole**

Niki Chesworth

The author of some 20 books on personal finance, Niki Chesworth has many years' experience of helping people make more of their money. Formerly money editor of 'The Express', she contributes regularly to the national press and broadcast media. Her down-to-earth approach and easy-to-understand style make her books essential for anyone who wants to take control of their money.

First published in 2000 by

Tesco Stores Limited

Created by Brilliant Books Ltd

84-86 Regent Street

London W1R 5PA

10 9 8 7 6 5 4 3 2 1

Origination by Graphic Ideas Studios Ltd, London

Printed and bound by Artes Gráficas, Toledo

D.L. TO: 1184-2000

This book has been written to help as many people as possible understand their financial needs. However, everyone's circumstances are different. Always read the small print before you sign any agreement or part with any money and, if you are in any doubt at all, consult a financial adviser.

Savings

& investments

contents

Saving sounds sensible – and it is. But try
thinking of it as a way to turn your dreams into
reality and it becomes much more attractive!

Getting started

You will probably earn upwards of £1 million during your working life. But how much of this will you have at the end of it? For most of us, the answer is 'very little'.

However, saving and investing some of your hard-earned cash can bring enormous benefits. It's not just about ensuring your long-term financial stability. It's also a way to safeguard your financial security today – giving you the comfort of knowing that, whatever life brings, you have a safety net to protect your financial position.

Saving and investing wisely can also help you to juggle your day-to-day finances – ensuring you have enough cash set aside to cope with an emergency, such as the boiler blowing up, without having to go begging to the bank.

It's also about making the most of your money. After all, why waste hundreds of pounds mishandling your overdraft, credit cards and loan repayments when you can save and invest to pay for things with cash?

And what about your hopes and dreams – a round-the-world trip, a sports car, a home abroad or your children's education? You can't pay for everything on the never-never. Sometimes the only way to afford what you want is to save up for it first.

Planning your savings and investments

Where do I start? The first step is to look at what you want to achieve. Don't be swayed by advertisements for high-rate savings accounts or discounts on charges for investment products until you have worked out exactly what you want from your savings or investments. Ask yourself the questions below.

Should I be saving and investing? The answer will generally be 'yes'. But if you have debts, such as an overdraft and/or outstanding credit-card balances, your priority should be to pay these off first. You are probably paying four or five times as much interest on these debts as you would earn on the same amount of cash in a savings account.

> **good** deals
>
> If you'd like information on savings products from Tesco, call the Tesco Personal Finance Helpline on **0845-710 40 10**.

Do I have enough 'safety-net' savings? If you lost your job, would you have enough set aside to pay your bills and feed yourself and your family? Ideally, you should have the equivalent of three months' outgoings in an easy-access savings account before you start considering saving and investing to achieve other goals.

What am I saving for in particular? Perhaps you want to save enough for a two-week holiday this summer or to move to a bigger home next year. If you make your goals attainable, you'll find them easier to achieve. Also, if you can see your money growing and your dream coming nearer to reality, you're more likely to stick to regular saving.

Unless you are lucky enough to be paid a large bonus at work or inherit some cash, the chances are that you won't have a large lump sum to invest. So your only option is to put away a little amount on a regular basis. Small sums can quickly build up into a sizeable amount of money. But be realistic. If you decide to save £100 a month in a regular savings scheme and then cannot afford it, you will quickly give up.

How much can I afford to set aside?

There's no point in thinking about investments, as opposed to straightforward saving, if you're not prepared to take a long-term view. With a savings scheme, your money is safe, but with an investment there is nearly always some risk that

How long can I leave my money invested for?

If your savings goals are realistic, and you can see your dream coming closer, you're more likely to stick to your savings plan

the value of your investments may fall if the stock market takes a tumble. If you are going to need your cash back after a year or two, you may be forced to sell at a bad time and could lose money. If you can wait until the market recovers, your investments will usually be profitable once again.

Am I prepared to take risks? If you are not prepared to risk the possibility that even £1 of your money could be lost, think twice about putting your cash into a stock market investment. However, it's also true that, over the longer term, your money may be at risk in a building society or bank savings account. If the rate of interest you earn after tax is less than the rate of inflation, your spending power in real terms will actually go down – in other words, your money will be worth less.

---

managing your savings and investments

You can't go wrong if you remember these basic rules:

- Invest little and often – you will hardly miss the money going out of your bank account each month, yet it will quickly grow into a sizeable sum.

- Leave your savings to grow – don't view them as a means of funding day-to-day extravagances.

- Ensure that your savings grow as much as possible by remembering to monitor their performance. A savings rate that is competitive today may not necessarily be the best on offer next month or next year. The same applies to other types of investment, such as ISAs.

- If you have invested in shares, only to see the stock market tumble, don't panic. The worst time to sell is when share prices are low. Be patient and wait for the recovery.

Getting financial advice

There are almost 1,000 savings accounts, almost 2,000 unit trust funds, more than 300 investment trusts and some 3,000 shares quoted on the London stock exchange. If you only want to save for the short term, then you can probably work out for yourself what types of product would be best for you. However, if you want to build up a nest egg for the longer term, and want to ensure you get the best buys and have the right spread of investments, getting financial advice is a good idea. It doesn't have to cost you a penny – and in some cases, it can even save you money.

Why do I need advice?

There's no shortage of companies offering financial advice. They range from high-street banks and building societies, to life insurance companies, stockbrokers, fund managers and firms of financial advisers. Shop around until you find an adviser you feel confident about and comfortable with.

Who can I go to for advice?

Independent financial advisers (IFAs) can recommend savings and investment products from a wide range of financial firms, whereas salesmen and women who work for just one company (usually known as investment or tied advisers) can recommend only the products of the company they work for. Most of the major banks and building societies are tied to a company offering investment products, but they may also have a division that offers independent financial advice.

Which type of adviser is best?

The first thing to be clear about is whether your adviser is offering independent financial advice or not. If you are unsure, ask. Also, check what experience the adviser has and

What questions should I ask an adviser?

which areas he or she specialises in. After all, there's no point talking to someone who only sells life insurance and pensions if you are thinking of investing in shares.

What questions will the adviser ask me?

The first thing the adviser should do is conduct a thorough fact-finding interview to find out what type of investor you are. That's why it will help to work through the questions on pages 8-10 before you meet an adviser. Some of the questions the adviser asks may seem a bit intrusive, but it's important that he or she knows as much about you as possible so the most suitable investments can be recommended. There is no point in taking out a 10-year savings plan, for instance, if you want to stop work and travel the world in three years' time.

How much does financial advice cost?

Financial advice doesn't have to cost a penny. This is because advisers often earn commission from the companies whose products they recommend. However, sometimes it's worth paying for an adviser's expertise – in return, the commission that would normally be paid to the adviser is invested in the product you buy. For smaller investments an adviser's fee may be more than this commission, but for larger investments it's certainly worth considering paying a fee.

Expect any financial adviser you use to question you closely about your goals and aspirations

If things go wrong

If a bank, building society or life company goes bust, there is a protection scheme in place to ensure that you get financial compensation. However, it's highly unlikely that any of the major financial firms will go under. If you're concerned about smaller financial companies and firms of financial advisers, there are protection schemes to ensure that, if a company goes bust while it holds your money, you can claim back your cash from the Investors' Compensation Scheme.

How do I know my money is safe?

If you think an unsuitable product was recommended to you or the risks were not clearly spelt out, first complain to the company that advised you. If you're not happy with the response, take your complaint to The Financial Services Authority (0845 606 1234). The FSA is the chief City watchdog for complaints against financial firms, such as life insurance companies, fund managers and investment advisers.

What if I'm unhappy with the advice I've been given?

In addition, there are several ombudsmen who can look into your complaint (but only if you have exhausted a company's in-house complaints procedure first) and award compensation where applicable. They are: The Banking Ombudsman (020 7404 9944), The Building Societies Ombudsman (020 7931 0044) and The Investment Ombudsman (020 7796 3065).

If you're unhappy with the way your savings or investment account is performing, there's little you can do other than take your money elsewhere. The watchdogs and ombudsmen will only look into cases where you've been given unsuitable advice or poor service. They won't compensate you because share prices fell or the fund manager didn't do a good job.

What can I do if my account underperforms?

When it comes to putting money aside for a rainy day, it's all too easy to underestimate just how much you and your family might need

Short-term savings

If you lost your job or were too ill to work, how long would your savings keep you going? As a nation we have lost the habit of saving. On average each of us has just £750 stashed away for a rainy day – hardly enough to keep a roof over our heads should disaster strike.

It's vital to have some savings – particularly if you're someone who tends to live right up to your overdraft and credit-card limits. If your bank won't let you borrow any more, you will need to have access to some emergency cash simply to help you cope with life's ups and downs.

Saving is a safe, non-speculative way of setting aside cash, while still earning a return in the form of interest. The amount your savings earn for you depends on the type of savings account you choose.

With almost a thousand accounts on offer from dozens of different institutions, ensuring you're getting the best deal is not always easy. The golden rule is to shop around before making your choice. Also, keep monitoring your account to check that it stays competitive: new accounts are launched every day, so just because you found the best deal a month or so ago, don't assume you still have the best deal today.

Choosing a savings account

What's an instant-access account?

An instant-access account is the simplest form of savings account – it allows you to pay in and withdraw your money whenever you want. These accounts offer you total flexibility, which makes them a good home for at least some of your safety-net savings, provided you can resist the temptation to raid the account for luxury spending.

However, flexibility may come at a price – interest rates on instant-access accounts run through bank and building society branches are often relatively low (although some are pretty competitive at the moment). Other types of accounts, such as notice accounts and savings bonds, offer less flexibility but, usually, much higher rates of interest.

What's a notice account?

A notice account requires you to give 30, 60, 75 or even 90 days' notice before you withdraw your money. Rates on notice accounts are often higher than on instant-access accounts, so they can offer you a good deal if you can plan

---

interest-bearing **current accounts**

Although it's better to earn some interest on your current account than no interest at all, don't be tempted to think of your current account as a savings account. The rates of interest paid on current accounts tend to be extremely low. If you need to keep a sizeable balance in your current account because you have to write out cheques for large amounts, consider opening a high-interest cheque account (HICA).

If you find it hard to resist raiding your savings, an account with restricted access can help to fight the temptation

ahead for withdrawals. The down side is that, if you need to withdraw money immediately, you could lose up to 90 days' interest (although some accounts let you make one penalty-free withdrawal a year). Also, you won't be able to switch accounts quickly if the rate doesn't remain competitive.

What's a savings bond?

A savings bond ties up your cash for a set period of time, often one or two years, and you'll usually have to invest a minimum amount of at least £1,000. The big plus point is that you'll receive a higher rate of interest than you would from other savings accounts. However, you'll pay a penalty (usually a loss of interest) if you take your money out early, so you need to be pretty sure you won't want the money for a while. Most savings bonds have a fixed interest rate, so if interest rates in general rise during the term of the bond you could find that the rate you're locked into is no longer competitive.

What about postal, internet or telephone accounts?

Bank and building society branches are expensive to run. It costs about 60p to process a transaction through a branch, but only 30p to process one by telephone, and just 10p on the internet. So if you save with an institution that doesn't have to pay for branches, such as a supermarket or internet bank, you can usually expect to earn a higher rate of interest. The same applies if you open an account with a bank or building society, but agree not to use their branch network.

If you want to withdraw money from a postal, telephone or internet account, you will usually be sent a cheque within days. Alternatively, cash may be transferred electronically to your current account, or issued via a cash machine.

What if I want to save on a regular basis?

Saving regularly is a very good habit to get into – and if you arrange to save the same amount of money each month, you're less likely to miss it. Many building societies and banks will reward you with higher rates if you make regular savings. Most savings accounts require you to make at least 12 consecutive payments, although some have a three-year term. The only drawback is, if you want to withdraw cash, some accounts charge a penalty, such as knocking 3% off your interest rate. The best accounts are the flexible ones that allow you up to three withdrawals a year without this affecting rates.

> **kids'** accounts
>
> Get your kids into the savings habit by opening a children's account. Most offer free perks, such as piggy banks or record vouchers, and some even give teenagers cash cards so they can withdraw money from cash machines. Remember to check that these accounts (which usually pay interest tax free) offer a reasonable rate of interest.

Nearly all of the rates on the top-paying savings accounts include a bonus – the only snag is that you have to keep your money invested for months to earn this bonus. But if you think you will be able to keep your money invested for a minimum period of time, an account with a bonus can give you the best of both worlds – instant access if you need your money in a hurry, and a higher rate of interest if you don't.

Are accounts that pay a bonus a good deal?

A few savings accounts now guarantee to track movements in general interest rates. The advantage of these accounts is that when rates go up you will benefit from the increase (with most types of savings account, some institutions fail to pass on interest rate rises in full or quickly). The drawback is that when rates fall, so will your savings rate.

What about accounts that track interest rates?

As a saver you don't necessarily need access to a branch network. Choose a postal account instead and you'll get a higher rate of interest

Which savings account is right for me?

Choosing a savings account is not just about looking at the advertised interest rate. Make sure the account offers you a good deal by asking the following questions:

- What's the rate of interest for the amount you want to save? Many accounts have tiered rates, with smaller sums earning a lower interest rate than larger deposits.
- What rate of interest would you earn if your savings dropped below a certain level? In some cases you won't earn a penny in interest if you have less than £500 saved, for example.
- What's the notice period? With some savings accounts you have to give 30 or 90 days' notice if you want to withdraw any of your money. If you want instant access to some or all of your cash, you could lose some of your interest.
- Do the best rates include a bonus? You may have to save on a regular basis or agree not to make any withdrawals for a certain length of time to qualify for a particular rate.
- How is the account operated? With some accounts you may have to deal by post, telephone or via the internet, rather than through a branch.

---

avoid the **pitfalls**

A few simple rules will help you make the most of your money:

- Don't withdraw large amounts – with less invested, the rate of interest you earn may drop sharply.
- Don't forget to monitor the interest rate on your account – if it drops, you may be better off putting your money elsewhere.
- Don't forget the notice period, otherwise you may withdraw cash only to find that you have lost interest as a result.
- Don't pay tax if you don't need to, either because you're a non-taxpayer (p23) or because you could have an ISA (p28).

'I was expecting to **double** my money'

When Claire Burgess's grandmother died in 1987 and left her £5,000, Claire's father put it in a deposit account at the local bank for the day she reached 18.

'I was only six at the time, and it seemed a lot of money to me,' says Claire, 18. 'I was told that when I grew up I would have enough cash for a deposit on my first home or to buy my first car.'

However, when Claire reached 18 and went to claim her inheritance, she was shocked to find that it had grown to less than £6,000 – just £3,000 in today's terms when you account for inflation. In the 12 years it had been in the bank, Claire's money had earned hardly any interest at all.

'I couldn't believe it,' says Claire. 'I was expecting at least double that amount and I'd already made plans to buy a car with the money. I was so disappointed.'

When her father had opened the account, interest rates had been in double figures, so Claire had assumed that she was earning a good rate of return. But the account her money had been left in had stopped being competitive years ago and was paying less than 1% interest by the time she reached 18. So, instead of her money growing, it was actually losing value in real terms – after taking inflation into account.

Claire has switched her cash to an account that pays six times as much interest, but she is still upset that, while she thought her money was safe because it was invested in savings, it wasn't, and she lost £2,000 of spending power as a result.

Understanding interest rates

What do gross interest and net interest mean?

Gross interest is the interest you earn on your savings before it is taxed. For most accounts the rate advertised is the gross rate. Net interest is what you get after the tax has been paid. You don't have to pay the tax yourself, though – if you are a taxpayer you will find tax is deducted from your interest automatically, leaving you with interest at the net rate.

What does AER mean?

Some interest rates are followed by the initials AER, which stands for Annual Equivalent Rate. The AER is often given for accounts where interest is paid monthly, and allows you to compare the rate with accounts paying interest annually. The AER shows what the interest rate would be if you left all your monthly interest in the account over the course of a year, allowing you to earn interest on the interest.

By the time you get the interest on your savings, the taxman may already have taken a share!

how savings are **taxed**

Basic-rate taxpayers If you're a basic-rate taxpayer tax is usually deducted from your interest before it is paid to you. For the tax year 2000/01, 20% of your gross (before-tax) interest will go to the Inland Revenue.

Lower-rate taxpayers If you only pay tax at the lower rate (10% on the first £1,500 of income for the tax year 2000/01), tax is still deducted at the 20% rate from your interest. However, you can reclaim the difference between the tax deducted and the tax you actually owe by contacting your local tax office.

Non-taxpayers If you're a non-taxpayer you can register to receive interest gross (without tax being deducted). You can do this by asking for form R85 at your bank or building society or by contacting your local tax office.

Higher-rate taxpayers All interest deducted from savings accounts is deducted at basic rate. If you pay tax at the higher rate you will need to declare the interest you have received from savings on your annual tax return and the Inland Revenue will collect the extra tax through your tax code.

Children In general children do not have to pay tax on the interest they earn from their savings. Make sure that you fill out form R85 when you open an account for a child. Parents cannot use their children's savings accounts to avoid paying tax themselves. If you pay money into your child's account and the child earns more than £100 in interest in a tax year, the Inland Revenue may tax this income as the parents' income. Asking grandparents and other relatives to contribute to your child's savings is one way to avoid this.

Joint savings accounts If you have a savings account in a joint name with your partner or spouse, the interest will usually be split 50/50 for tax purposes.

Does it matter when interest is credited? Even if your account adds interest only at the end of the year, if you withdraw your savings part of the way through the year you'll usually be credited with interest for the number of days your money has been in the account. The main advantage of having interest paid more often is that you can then earn interest on the interest. Some accounts pay interest monthly for those who rely on their savings to supplement their income.

How do I know that I'm getting a good rate? It is up to you to keep a close eye on your savings rate – the rate that attracted you to an account may not remain competitive for long. Often banks and building societies offer new accounts with high rates of interest to attract new savers, leaving existing customers earning a poorer return. Being prepared to move your money around means you are more likely to get a better rate.

All financial institutions that offer savings accounts have to advertise when interest rates change and write to people with postal accounts telling them of any changes. But they're under no obligation to tell you that you're no longer getting the best deal. They must also write to all savers at least once a year telling them what rate they've been earning and what interest rates are being offered on their other accounts.

---

discontinued accounts

If your bank or building society replaces the type of account you have with a new type, the rate on your original account must either be kept at a comparable level to the new account or you should be able to switch to a new account that has similar features. If there is no account available that's similar to yours, you must be informed within 30 days so that you can decide what to do with your money.

To earn a good rate of interest you need to keep a careful eye on exactly what's on offer

The easiest way to earn more interest on your savings is to shop around. Also, you can often get a higher rate if you:

How can I get a better rate?

Invest a larger amount However, don't assume that a large sum means a high rate of interest. Check what rates of interest the account pays for different amounts.

Tie up your cash for longer Agree to a 30-, 60- or 90-day notice period or lock into a one-, two- or three-year savings bond.

Save for a set period Invest either in a bond – which requires you to tie up your cash for one or two years – or in an account that pays a bonus if you keep your money invested for a year or until some other set date.

Make fewer transactions Some banks and building societies will reward you if you don't make many transactions. For example, you could get a bonus if you make fewer than two withdrawals a year or no more than five.

Invest regularly You can often earn more interest by making regular payments into your savings account.

Avoid bank or building society branch networks Opt for accounts that are run by post, telephone or internet – these types of account usually offer a much better rate of interest.

Don't let the taxman get his hands on your interest. Use your tax-free savings entitlement and you can keep more of it for yourself

Tax-free saving

How can you turn £80 of interest into £100? The answer is to save in a tax-free scheme, such as an Individual Savings Account (ISA). That way, you get to keep the £20 that would normally go to the Inland Revenue as tax.

More than half the UK adult population have a bank or building society savings account, yet only a fifth have a tax-free savings account. As a result we are paying an estimated £1 billion in unnecessary tax. Savings interest is usually paid with tax already deducted, so you may not realise that you're paying money to the taxman when you don't need to.

If you're a higher-rate taxpayer you're losing even more. Of every £100 you earn in interest, you will keep just £60 unless you make use of the tax-free schemes on offer. Even if you're a non-taxpayer, you could still be losing out. Some five million 'non-taxpayers' allow their savings to be taxed because they haven't registered for tax-free interest.

Tax-free savings schemes are as easy to open as ordinary accounts – and they often pay a better rate of interest as well – so what are you waiting for?

Cash ISAs

What is a cash ISA? A cash ISA is one element of the tax-free savings scheme introduced by the government in April 1999. The scheme gives most taxpayers the chance to save and invest a certain amount each year tax free. A cash ISA is similar to an ordinary savings account, but the interest you earn is tax free.

How much can I save in a cash ISA? You can invest a maximum £3,000 cash in an ISA within the current tax year (from 6 April to 5 April), dropping to £1,000 from April 2001. But you can only use your investment allowance once each year. So, if you invest £3,000 in savings, then withdraw £3,000, you cannot reinvest the cash during the same tax year because you will already have used your £3,000 limit for that year.

Is a cash ISA right for me? Almost certainly yes. Why pay tax on your savings if you don't have to? Even if you are a non-taxpayer, you may find a cash ISA offers a more competitive rate of interest than other savings accounts. However, before you start a cash ISA, you need to understand what other types of ISA are available and what your ISA limits are for each year (see page 31).

How do I know if I'm getting a good deal? Look out for ISAs that meet the government's CAT standard. This stands for low Charges, easy Access and fair Terms. The CAT rules vary, depending on what you are investing in. For cash savings the rules are as follows:
- No one-off or regular charges of any kind – so that means no charges for withdrawals or for any regular service, such as a statement. However, charges for lost cards, duplicate statements and other similar services are allowed.

There are lots of possible homes for your tax-free savings. ISA accounts that meet the CAT standard usually offer a good deal

- The minimum transaction limit must be no higher than £10 and any money paid into the account must be credited within seven working days or less.
- The interest rate must be no lower than 2% below base rate.
- Interest rates must be increased within a calendar month of the Bank of England increasing base rates, although changes may be slower if the base rate moves downwards.

It's worth pointing out that some ISAs that do not meet these CAT standards can still offer a good deal. For example, they may require a higher minimum deposit or longer notice, but still offer very competitive rates.

ISAs: minis and maxis

There are three main types of investment allowed under the ISA tax-free savings scheme: cash savings, share-based investments, and life insurance investments. Each of these may be held in either mini ISAs or a maxi ISA – each mini ISA can hold only one of the three types of investments, whereas a maxi ISA may contain up to three different types of investment.

Annual limits In each tax year (a year running from 6 April to 5 April) you are allowed to buy only one maxi ISA or three different types of mini ISA – but not both mini and maxi ISAs.

There are strict limits on how much you're allowed to invest in each type of ISA this year and in future years from April 2001. (Figures in brackets are new limits for the 2001-2002 tax year.)

Mini ISAs	or	**Maxi ISA**
Mini cash ISA: up to £3,000 (£1,000)		Up to £7,000 in stocks and shares (£5,000) **or** Up to £4,000 in stocks and shares plus £3,000 in cash **or** Up to £5,000 in stocks and shares, plus £1,000 in cash and £1,000 in life insurance
+		
Mini stocks and shares ISA: up to £3,000 (£3,000)		
+		
Mini life insurance ISA: up to £1,000 (£1,000)		

Once you have invested your ISA limit you have used it up for the year. You cannot take your money out and then reinvest it; once you sell all or part of an ISA investment, that particular tax-free allocation is lost for ever.

This depends on whether or not you want to invest in stocks and shares through an ISA as well as save. If you only want to save cash, then it doesn't matter whether you choose a mini or a maxi ISA – your annual limit for cash savings is £3,000 in either type of account. However, if you open a mini ISA you cannot open a maxi ISA in the same year. So if you want to invest more than you want to save, you may be better off with a maxi ISA, which lets you invest more in stocks and shares than a mini ISA (see opposite).

Is a mini ISA or a maxi ISA best for me?

From a bank, building society or other savings account provider, such as a supermarket.

Where can I buy an ISA?

If you're unhappy with the performance of your ISA, you can switch to another provider – but you will have to stick to the same kind of investment. So you can switch a mini cash ISA from one provider to another, but you cannot switch a mini cash ISA into a mini stocks and shares ISA. If you switch provider, make sure your money is transferred directly between ISAs, rather than closing one ISA then opening another.

What if I'm unhappy with my ISA?

---

the **ISA** basics

The key features of the ISA tax-free savings scheme are:

- The money you make on your ISA investments will not be subject to income tax or capital gains tax. You do not have to declare your ISA income and gains on your tax return.
- You can get money out at any time without losing tax relief.
- You have to be aged 18 or over and resident in the UK.
- You can only hold an ISA in your own name and cannot have a joint account with someone else.

Tax-Exempt Special Savings Accounts (TESSAs)

What is a TESSA? TESSA stands for Tax-Exempt Special Savings Account. These were withdrawn from sale in April 1999 and replaced by ISAs. However, as TESSAs have a five-year term, thousands of investors are still paying into their TESSAs each year.

What should I do with my TESSA? If you can afford to, keep paying in up to the limits allowed. You could have invested up to £3,000 in year one, and up to £1,800 in years two to five, bearing in mind that total contributions for the five-year period cannot exceed £9,000.

Don't cash in your TESSA unless you desperately need the money. Once you've cashed it in you cannot open another one and will have lost this particular tax-free savings allowance for good. If you do need some money you can withdraw the interest you've earned, leaving the capital you invested, and still keep your TESSA going. However, the tax element of your interest has to stay in your account if you withdraw any before the end of the five-year term. Once your TESSA matures after five years, move it into a TESSA-only ISA. You can only transfer the capital you have invested up to the maximum of £9,000 and not any of the interest you have earned.

What if I'm not happy with my TESSA? You can switch from one TESSA provider to a new one, but the money must be transferred directly from one company to the other. Some providers charge penalties – a £25-plus switching fee or up to 90 days' loss of interest if you want to move your money elsewhere. And there are some providers that will not accept transfers into their accounts from other providers.

'I'm amazed how **much** I can save'

Having climbed the career ladder successfully, Jason Dawson was keen to start saving and investing but didn't want to give a large slice of the interest to the tax man.

'I've already paid 40% tax on my income, so I don't want to invest it and then pay 40% tax on any interest I get,' says Jason, 42, from Manchester.

'I've had a portfolio of stock market investments for some time and they're performing well. But, as our two daughters are approaching five and seven and we want to educate them privately, I also need to have some money in less long-term schemes – cash I will be able to withdraw once a term to pay the school fees. That's why I've started investigating tax-free savings plans. I'm amazed how much I can save, totally tax free.'

Before TESSAs were abolished Jason started a scheme with £3,000. He's now put in another £3,600 and can carry on topping up the account for a further two years until he has £9,000 saved. 'It's earning a good rate of interest and, more importantly, it's tax free,' says Jason. 'It will mature just when I'll be needing a cash lump sum.'

When ISAs were introduced Jason took out a mini cash ISA, taking advantage of the introductory allowance of £3,000 in cash. The next year, he invested another £3,000, and when the investment limits drop he intends to make use of the £1,000 allowance for at least two more years. 'By the time our eldest starts private school at age 11, I'll have at least £17,000 in tax-free savings to pay for the first years of her education.'

National Savings

What do National Savings offer? National Savings offer a number of tax-free saving options, including Index-linked Certificates, Savings Certificates and a cash ISA. National Savings Premium Bonds are not strictly a savings account but they do pay out prizes tax free. The prize fund is equivalent to the rate of interest that would be earned on an average savings account.

What are Index-linked Certificates? Index-linked Certificates pay a rate of interest fixed above the rate of inflation. They require a minimum investment of £100 and have a two-year or five-year term. Interest is not taxed. However, if you withdraw your money within the first year, you will receive no interest at all.

Index-linked Certificates are a good way to protect your savings from inflation, but if earning interest is your priority you'll probably be able to get a better deal elsewhere, even when you take the certificates' tax-free status into account.

What are Savings Certificates? Savings Certificates pay a fixed rate of interest for a set term – either two or five years – and have a minimum investment of £100. Interest is not taxed. If you withdraw your cash before the term is up you could get reduced interest, with no interest paid if you withdraw your money in the first year.

If you think interest rates are as high as they're going to go, or are about to start falling, then Savings Certificates offer you a way to lock into high rates of interest tax free. However, if interest rates rise once you've put money into Savings Certificates, you'll lose out if you want to switch your cash to an account with a more competitive rate.

Index-linked Certificates offer you an interest rate that's linked to inflation – if inflation rises, then so does the interest your savings earn

National Savings do have tax advantages, but the rates aren't usually as competitive as the best on the high street, so make sure you use up your ISA allowance before opting for this form of saving. Once the set term for your Index-linked and Savings Certificates is up, reinvest in new ones or move your money to a new savings account. If you leave your money with National Savings after the term is up, it will earn only the 'general extension rate' – a very low rate of interest.

Are National Savings right for me?

---

offshore savings

Most of the major banks and building societies have offshore subsidiaries in the Isle of Man, Guernsey or Jersey. These accounts pay interest gross, but you are still liable to pay tax on this interest and should declare it to the Inland Revenue.

Even if you are a non-taxpayer you'll probably find that you haven't really got a very good deal. Many offshore accounts pay comparatively low rates of interest, so you are usually better off putting your money in a UK savings account that offers a competitive rate of interest.

The stock market is not for the faint-hearted.
But if you're ready to ride the ups and downs, it can
produce great returns for longer-term investors

Longer-term investments

A savings account may provide a safe home for your cash in the short term, but over the longer term you could see the real value of your money eroded by inflation.

Even if you pick a savings account that has a decent rate of interest, you may only just beat inflation. Over the past five years, £1,000 invested in a savings account would have had to grow to £1,150 to maintain your spending power, and yet the average account has grown to only £1,200 – just £50 more. If, however, you'd put the same money in the stock market, it would be worth, on average, around £2,345. While it may be rewarding to earn 5% on your savings, why make do with that when you could be earning 10% or even 20%?

The only drawback is that, if you want to take advantage of the greater opportunities offered by the stock market, you will have to be prepared to take a certain amount of risk with your money. You can, however, reduce the risks by spreading them – buying a wider range of shares – and investing for the longer term so that your money can ride out any rises and falls in the stock market. Remember, while shares tend to produce better returns than savings in the long term, stock markets do not rise in a straight line.

Understanding the stock market

What is the stock market? The stock market is much like any market – a place where goods are bought and sold. On the stock market, it's shares, rather than actual goods, that are traded.

Why is it important to me? Virtually everyone has an exposure to the stock market – if you are a member of a company pension scheme, some of your future security depends on the performance of shares. The same applies if you have a personal pension, an endowment policy or a savings plan that invests in shares. In addition, 12 million private investors own shares directly.

What does it mean when the stock market rises and falls? It means that the value of the companies listed on the stock market has risen or fallen. If it falls, it is usually because of general concerns about the state of the economy, such as fears that interest rates will rise, poor export figures or a less optimistic outlook. If the stock market rises, it is usually because the economy is doing well and therefore there are expectations that companies quoted on the stock market will produce bigger profits and dividends (dividends are the income paid to shareholders).

How can I keep track of its performance? Movements in the stock market are reported regularly on the television and radio as well as in all the newspapers.

Markets fall in 'points', which shouldn't be confused with percentages. You may hear on the news that 120 points were wiped off the share index, but if the share index is 6000, this amounts to only 2%.

Ultimately it is the investor who determines what happens to the stock market. Most stock market investments are held by the large pension funds and life insurance companies, who invest billions of pounds on behalf of their customers. If these investors move large amounts of money out of shares and into other investments – such as deposits that are safer – demand for shares drops and so does the price.

However, it is stockbrokers who determine day-to-day movements in prices. They employ market analysts and economists who forecast the prospects for the economy and for individual companies listed on the stock market, and recommend if individual shares should be bought or sold.

Who controls the stock market?

A stock market is like any other market: a place where goods are bought and sold – in this case, shares in the ownership of different companies

Do world events affect the stock market?

Yes – we are in a global market, so the stock market doesn't just depend on what happens here in the UK – it's also influenced by what happens in every market around the world. So, for example, if a Latin American or Eastern European country is finding it difficult to repay its international debts, this in turn can hit global bank shares and lead to a crisis of confidence, which can ultimately cause crashes in stock markets all around the world.

If I invest in the stock market will I always make money?

Yes and no. It's true that, in most five-year periods since the Second World War, the stock market has produced positive returns that not only beat inflation but also provide higher rates of return than savings accounts.

However, you have to remember that stock markets do not rise in a straight line. They rise and fall on a daily basis and sometimes the trend is downwards. If you buy a stock market based investment or an individual share when the market is at a peak, and it falls in value, you will obviously lose money if you then decide to sell your investment.

---

stock market terms

Quoted company A quoted company is any company that is listed (or trading) on the stock market.

Blue-chip shares These are shares in large, solid companies in the FTSE 100. They tend to be less volatile than other shares and are popular with investors who want to limit their risks.

Tracker funds These are investment funds that aim to track a stock market index – usually the FTSE 100 or the All Share Index. They're popular because many investment funds fail to match the performance of the stock market as a whole.

How shares are traded

A share is simply a legal document that gives the person who holds it part-ownership of the company that issues the share. Companies issue shares to raise finance. There are different types of share available (see page 45), each of which gives the shareholder different rights. However, most shares owned by private investors are straightforward ordinary shares.

What's a share?

Share prices on the stock market change second by second throughout the trading day. The price of shares depends on supply and demand. The more investors who want to buy a particular share, the bigger the increase in the value of that share. The more who want to sell a particular share, the further its price will fall. Share prices are also affected by the state of the economy and forecasts for its growth, government policy and interest rates, how well a particular sector is performing, the management of a company and its profits.

What affects the price of shares?

The UK stock market is divided into several listings. The best known is the 'Footsie' or the FTSE (Financial Times Stock Exchange) 100 Index, made up of the 100 largest companies by value whose shares are traded on the UK stock market.

What is the Footsie?

Other indices are the FTSE 250 (the 250 largest companies by share value) and the All Share Index (all companies listed on the UK stock market). There is also a sort of junior stock market – the Alternative Investment Market (AIM) – where companies hoping to get a full listing on the main stock market can float initially. A flotation is when a company joins the stock market and starts to sell its shares.

What other listings are there?

Buying individual shares

How can I make money out of shares?

The main way to make money from shares is to buy them and then sell them at a higher price than you originally paid. Not all of the difference will be profit, though – you'll have to pay dealing costs, stamp duty and, sometimes, tax.

The other way to make money is by earning dividends. This is money paid to shareholders, usually every six months, and is a share of a company's profits for a certain period.

Who buys shares?

Although there are 12 million private shareholders in the UK, most of them own only a few shares, perhaps from a privatisation in the 1980s or, more recently, from a building society demutualisation. However, there is a growing number of private investors who are taking advantage of new technology to trade regularly on the internet at low cost and with access to the latest market information.

More and more people, from all walks of life, are following the market and investing in shares

Share buying is only for you if you are prepared to take a risk and are able to take a long-term view. It's risky because the value of a share can fall as well as rise, so you are not guaranteed to get all your money back when you sell. You need to be able to invest for the long term, so that if the price of a share tumbles you can hold on to your investment until the price recovers. If you think you may panic and sell at a loss, then perhaps share buying is not for you.

Is share buying right for me?

There are other less risky ways of investing in the stock market – see Collective Investments (pages 52-61).

You can keep up to date with stock market news by reading newspapers and magazines. Many investment advisers will recommend that you stick to what you know – if you concentrate on investing in companies you are familiar with you'll find it a lot easier to track their performance.

How do I know if a share is worth buying?

If you want advice on which shares to buy you can go to a stockbroker, but this may be expensive and you usually need to have an investment of at least £10,000 to make it worth while. If you feel that you don't need advice on which shares to buy, then you have several options:

Where can I buy shares?

- Your bank/building society may offer a share-dealing service, although it may be restricted to the top 100 companies.
- You can go to a stockbroker for an 'execution-only' or broking service. Transactions will usually be conducted by telephone or post, which makes this cheaper than going through a bank or building society.
- You can buy shares via the internet, although you'll need to set up an account with an appropriate service. Simply type in 'share dealing' on your search engine to find a site.

As a shareholder you'll usually have the right to attend a company's annual general meetings and vote on how the company is run

How much does it cost to buy a share? Dealing costs, whether through a stockbroker or via the internet, start at around £15. However, for this price you won't get any advice on which shares to buy. In addition to the dealing costs, you'll have to pay stamp duty of 0.5% of the value of the shares you buy.

You should also be aware that there is a difference between the buying price and selling price of a share; this is known as the bid-offer spread. The price at which a share is offered and at which you buy it is usually around 1-5% higher than the price at which you can sell the same share. The price quoted for the share in a newspaper will be the mid price – halfway between the buying and selling price. This extra charge is not uncommon in finance – there is a similar spread when you buy and sell foreign currency.

Dealing costs mean it is not normally economic to buy less than £500 of shares. If you want to buy only £100 of shares, 20% of your investment could go in costs. One way to get around this is to invest in a unit or investment trust (see pages 54-61), where costs are shared among hundreds of investors.

You will usually need to open an account with a stockbroker or broking service so that money can be transferred in and out when you sell or buy shares. You pay for your shares on settlement day, usually five days after the trade takes place (although this is due to be reduced to three days).

How do I pay for my shares?

different types of **share**

Certificated You receive a share certificate, which you need to present when you sell the shares. You appear on the company's share register and have the right to receive dividends and to attend and vote at annual general meetings of the company.

Nominee The growth of electronic trading (without share certificates) means you now have the option of having your shares held in a nominee account by a broker. You are the actual owner of the shares, but do not receive a share certificate or appear on the company's register of shareholders. Your rights to dividends are the same as if you held the share certificate, but you cannot vote as other shareholders do and you may miss out on shareholder information (such as the annual report) and any shareholder perks (see page 49).

Crest Trading through Crest, the settlement system for UK shares, allows you to pay for your shares quickly and easily. Your shares will be held in electronic form, but you will still have the same rights as if you held an actual certificate. You can usually become a sponsored member of Crest by paying a fee of around £10 to your stockbroker.

How do I keep track of the share prices? If you are a private investor, especially one investing for the long term, you probably don't need access to the kind of up-to-the-minute information that professional dealers require. However, it is important to know how well your shares or share-based investments are performing and how well the stock market is doing in general, so that you don't sell when prices are low or buy when they're high.

Share prices for individual companies quoted on the stock market are listed in most newspapers. Changes in the total value of the different listings are also given and shown as a rise and fall in points. Share prices are also posted on the internet.

When you look up a share price, you'll probably find quoted companies divided into sectors, such as retail and banking, to make it easier to find the one you're looking for. If you are about to buy or sell shares, don't forget that prices may have changed in the few hours since the newspaper was printed or the information posted on the internet.

Judging the right moment to sell your shares will make all the difference to your profits

'I have **stakes** in five big companies'

Like many shareholders, Kate Flaunders, a catering supervisor from Macclesfield, has only a vague idea of how the stock market works, yet she has still been lucky enough to make money from buying shares.

'Like lots of people, I invested in a couple of privatisations in the mid-1980s, mainly to make a quick profit,' admits Kate, 38. 'Then, a couple of years ago, I received some windfall shares when my building society converted to a bank. I decided I wanted to know more about whether I should sell them quickly in case the price went down, or hold on to them.' That's when Kate started to follow the share columns in newspapers.

'I quickly discovered that I would be better off keeping hold of my shares. But that wasn't all. I read that the company I worked for was a potential takeover target. I know this company like the back of my hand and thought it was a good investment, so I bought some shares. Since then, I haven't looked back. I now have stakes in five big companies. But I'm in there for the long term – these shares are definitely not a quick punt or a gamble.

'Naturally, if one of the shares I own suddenly soared in price and I didn't think that the rise would last, I would cash in and take my profits. And I do monitor the performance of my shares so that if one's not doing well I may switch to another. But I won't take my money out of the stock market. I'm completely convinced that investing in shares is the best way to make money over the long term.'

how shares are **taxed**

You can be taxed on both the profit you make when you sell your shares and any income you get in the form of dividends. Whether you are taxed or not depends on how much you make and whether or not you are a taxpayer.

How profits are taxed Profits on shares are taxed under capital gains tax rules, which are quite complex. In any one tax year (which runs from 6 April to 5 April), you are allowed to make up to a certain amount of profit tax free. For the 2000/2001 tax year, the limit is £7,200. A married couple can effectively pool their individual allowances.

Your profit is not what you sell your shares for, but the sale price minus the purchase price and any costs such as dealing charges. For gains over the tax threshold, there's a percentage that's tax free (depending on the number of years you have held your shares). Tax on the rest is charged at lower, basic or higher rate, depending on your annual income.

How dividends are taxed When you receive your dividend, a 10% tax credit will already have been deducted. If you are a lower- or basic-rate taxpayer, you will not have to pay any more tax. If you are a higher-rate taxpayer, you'll have to pay further tax to take the total tax on the dividend up to the higher rate. Non-taxpayers cannot reclaim the 10% tax that has been paid.

How to avoid paying tax Invest in tax-free schemes (see pages 62-69 for more details). Alternatively, take out an investment, such as a bond fund, that pays an income rather than a dividend. That way, if you are a non-taxpayer, you can earn your income tax free. Taxpayers – who tend to be earners and therefore may not need investment income – should opt for shares that grow rather than those that pay a high dividend. This is because it is easier to escape paying tax on your profits than on any income.

As a shareholder in, say, a hotel chain, you
could be entitled to perks such as a discount
on your room tariff and a free room upgrade

Some companies offer extra incentives to encourage their **What are** sharcholders to become customers and to promote loyalty. **shareholder** The number of shares you need to purchase to qualify varies. **perks?**

If you regularly use a particular company or its products, you **Why buy a** may want to buy some shares so that you can get a discount **share with** on all your spending. For example, if you regularly eat in a **a perk?** particular chain of restaurants, buying just a few shares may bring you free meals or money-off vouchers.

It's only worth buying shares just for the perk if the perk is **Is it worth** so good that it outweighs any losses you may make on the **buying just for** share. For example, if buying a share gives you a 10% discount **the perk?** on holidays and you are planning an expensive long-haul trip, the perk could be worth more than the cost of the shares plus any losses you might suffer in the short term.

share **clubs**

A share club is a club set up by a group of colleagues or friends to pool cash so that they have greater buying power on the stock market and can share expertise and ideas.

Anyone over 18 can set up a club. Usually there are between two and 20 members. A constitution should be drawn up stating how much members will invest each month. Pick a figure that everyone can afford – the average is about £25 to £30 a month. The constitution should also cover what happens if someone wants to leave. For information on setting up a club, call ProShare (UK) Ltd on 020 7394 5200.

What else do I need to know? There are five main rules to investing in the stock market:

Weigh up the risks and the rewards In general, the greater the risk you take, the greater the potential rewards. So, if you invest in an unknown internet company with no track record, you will be taking a high risk. You could lose all your cash, but on the other hand you could reap huge rewards.

Diversify Buy across a range of sectors to ensure that you aren't caught out by slumps in one sector. This is why many share clubs manage to do so well – by pooling cash they can invest in a wider range of shares.

Buy cheap and sell expensive It's not always easy to do, but try to buy when a share's price is low and sell when it's high.

Do your research The more you can find out about the shares, the company, its products and its market, the better chance you have of picking a winner.

Invest for the long term If you haven't got the nerve or the funds to stick with a share through the bad times, you don't stand a chance of being there for the good times.

Employee share schemes

Millions of workers become shareholders for the first time by joining their company's employee share scheme. The most popular type is the SAYE (save as you earn) scheme. These schemes, which must offer shares to all employees, give staff the right – but not the obligation – to buy shares in the company they work for. Usually you would agree to buy shares at a certain price and then invest a regular amount (from £5 to £250 a month) over three, five or seven years. At the end of this period you have the option to buy the shares at the agreed price, or withdraw your savings plus interest.

What is an employee share scheme?

These schemes are usually a good deal. You may well be offered shares at a discount of up to 20% of the share's actual value – so even if the value doesn't rise, you still stand to make money. As you don't actually buy your shares for several years, the chances are that the share price will rise and you'll end up buying them for much less than they're worth.

Are they worth investing in?

With an Approved Profit Sharing (APS) scheme, your employer gives you shares representing part of the company's profits. The shares are held in trust for two years. After this, if you don't sell them for a further year, you won't have to pay any tax on the money you make. After 2002 the APS will be replaced by a new scheme under which employers can give employees up to £3,000 worth of shares each year free of tax.

What's an APS scheme?

Usually only open to senior management, a share option scheme offers the right to buy shares between three and 10 years ahead at the market price when the option is granted.

What's a share option scheme?

How collective investments work

What is a collective investment? Collective or pooled investments are exactly what they sound like – the money of hundreds if not thousands of investors collected together and invested in share-based investments.

What are the advantages? The more money there is in a fund, the wider the spread of investments can be – and therefore the wider the risk is spread. So, for example, if you invest in just one or two shares and they do badly, you can lose a substantial chunk of your money. However, if you invest in 50 or even 100 different shares, the risk of losing money is greatly reduced.

Another benefit is that the cost of investing is shared. Buy shares alone and you have to pay all the dealing costs. Buy your shares along with hundreds of other investors and dealing costs are shared out, making collective investments one of the cheapest ways to invest in the stock market.

Finally when you buy into a collective investment you also buy into the expertise of a fund management company. The fund management company makes all the investment decisions, which saves you having to decide which shares to buy.

The amount you can pay into a collective investment varies from scheme to scheme, but it can be as little as £20 to £50 a month or £250 to £500 as a lump sum.

Are there any disadvantages? Collective investments don't automatically produce a good return, with many of them failing to match the performance of the stock market. You have to pick the right fund and fund management company – that's why it can pay to get advice.

Collective investments include funds managed by pension and life companies, but the main types that appeal to investors are known as unit trusts and investment trusts. These are discussed in more detail on pages 54-61.

What types of collective investment are there?

If you already have some savings and want to start investing in the stock market without the risk of investing in shares directly, then collective investments could be right for you. Different schemes have different investment aims, so there should be one that appeals to you whether you are looking for capital growth, a regular income, long-term financial security or a shorter-term profit.

Are they right for me?

If you are new to the stock market and are nervous about the risks, collective investments are a good way to test the water

Unit trusts

What is a unit trust?

A unit trust is an investment fund made up of the money of hundreds of investors. The fund is split into units of equal value, which investors buy. The value of the units rises and falls depending on how well the money in the fund is invested. In the UK around £240 billion is invested in unit trusts.

What types of unit trust are there?

Unit trusts are split into sectors, according to the type of investments they hold and what their investment aims are. A UK growth fund, for example, will invest in UK shares with the aim of making your money grow rather than providing you with an income. The main sectors are UK Equity Income, UK All Companies, UK General Bonds, Europe excluding the UK, Global Growth and North America.

How do I know which unit trust to buy?

There are almost 2,000 unit trust funds, each with different investment goals, different charges, different minimum investments and different management expertise, so you may well want to seek financial advice before investing.

If you've never invested before, you can visit an independent financial adviser who will guide you through the options, or you can pick one of the lower-risk funds that invest in a broad range of shares across sectors and regions.

If you feel confident about picking your own investment without advice, you can buy direct from the fund management company or through a discount broker (see page 56).

Which types are the most popular?

Different types of investment tend to go in and out of favour depending on how well a sector performs. Tracker funds, which track a stock market index such as the FTSE 100, have

Some funds are now managed by computer programs, making human fund managers an unnecessary expense

been popular recently because they have low charges and perform as well as the stock market (something many unit trusts fail to do). These funds are managed by computer programs, rather than expensive fund managers, so the charges tend to be far lower than for many other unit trusts.

Bond funds have also been popular recently. A bond, such as a corporate bond, is similar to a share in that it is issued by companies to raise finance. Bonds are traded much like shares, but instead of paying a dividend they pay a rate of interest over the lifetime of the bond. Bond funds provide investors with an income rather than long-term growth. Although the income they pay can be high, the capital (initial investment) can be eroded.

You can invest from as little as £50 a month or £500 as a lump sum. There are a few unit trust companies that will accept even lower amounts.

How much do I need to invest?

How long do I need to invest for?

In theory you can buy a unit trust today and sell it tomorrow if you have to, without any penalties. However, as around 5% of your investment may be deducted in charges, you will be instantly worse off. You should aim to hold on to your investment for at least three to five years, so that you ride out any rises and falls in share prices and cover your costs.

What are the costs of investing?

There are two main charges: the initial charge and the annual management charge. The initial charge is deducted when you first invest and can be anything from 1% to 5%, although a few funds have no initial charge. The annual management charge can range from 0.25% to 1.75%.

> **discount** deals
>
> If you buy a unit trust through a discount broker, some of the initial charge (which usually goes as commission to the person who sells the unit trust) will be rebated to you. This can be up to £180 on a £3,000 investment.

How are unit trusts priced?

Units have two prices: a buying or offer price, which you pay when you purchase your units, and a bid or selling price, which you receive when you sell your units. The difference between the two, known as the bid-offer spread, can be as much as 6%. If you look up the value of your units in a newspaper, what you will see is the mid price – halfway between the two. The difference between the prices represents a combination of the initial charge, sales commission and other costs. The usual spread is around 5%.

What are the risks?

There is some risk that you could lose part of your initial investment, but only if you sell when share prices in general have fallen and therefore the value of your units is lower. That is why you should only invest cash that you are prepared to leave untouched for several years. If the stock market falls, you can wait until it recovers before selling.

Another risk is picking a sector that performs badly. In 1998, for example, Far Eastern funds fell dramatically, with many halving in value. You need to be in a position to wait until a sector recovers (as the Far East did by the end of 1999) rather than having to sell when the value of your units is low.

Unit trusts are generally taxed in the same way as shares (see page 48): you pay capital gains tax on your profits above a certain level and your dividend income is paid net of tax. The one exception is for bond funds, on which non-taxpayers can reclaim the tax that is automatically deducted and 10% tax-payers can claim back some of the tax. You needn't worry about tax at all if you invest through an ISA (pages 64-71).

How will I be taxed?

You can get more information by contacting the Association of Unit Trusts and Investment Funds on 020 8207 1361.

How can I find out more?

All about **OEICs**

An Open-Ended Investment Company (OEIC, pronounced 'oik') is usually a unit trust that has converted to a company. Instead of managing dozens of unit trusts, fund managers only have to deal with one umbrella OEIC with several different sub-funds.

For investors this can mean it's easier to switch from fund to fund. In addition, there's no difference between the buying and selling price, making them easier to understand. Although there is no bid-offer spread, charges still have to be paid separately, so they aren't any cheaper to invest in.

Investment trusts

What is an investment trust?

An investment trust is a listed company that invests in other companies in the UK and around the world. The trust employs fund managers who decide which companies to invest in. Individual investors buy into these investments by purchasing shares in the trust. Investment trusts have a fixed number of shares that are traded on the stock exchange, where their price fluctuates according to supply and demand.

There is around £80 billion invested in more than 330 investment trusts. The bulk of these investments is made by large institutional investors, such as pension funds and life insurance companies, but even so there are around 750,000 private shareholders in investment trusts in the UK alone.

What types of investment trust are there?

Some investment trusts have a general brief and invest in a broad range of UK shares and investments worldwide – this accounts for 50% of the money managed by investment trusts. Others specialise in one particular investment sector or geographical area. In addition, some investment trusts aim to generate income while others emphasise capital growth, and some offer a combination of the two.

Some investment trusts, known as split capital trusts, have different types of share – capital shares and income shares – to cater for different investment needs. If you want to invest in these or another specialist investment trust, you should seek independent financial advice first.

How much do I need to invest?

Investment trusts enable investors to start building up a stock market portfolio with as little as £25 a month. The minimum lump sum investment is usually £250.

As with all share-based investments, you should aim to hold your shares for a minimum of three to five years to cover costs and allow you to ride out any falls in the stock market. However, you can sell your shares at any time.

How long do I need to invest for?

Low costs are a feature of investment trust companies. In many cases the annual management charge is 0.5% or less of what you invest. In addition, as with the purchase of shares in any company, you will have to pay government stamp duty of 0.5% of the value of the transaction.

What are the costs of investing?

One of the cheapest ways to buy shares can be through an investment trust savings scheme, which can be used to invest lump sums as well as for regular savings.

Thanks to investment trusts, almost anyone can afford to invest in the stock market. Some require a minimum monthly investment of just £25

How do I buy investment trust shares? If you feel confident about choosing a company you can invest either directly through the investment trust's regular savings scheme or by buying shares via a stockbroker (dealing charges start at around £15).

Alternatively, visit an independent financial adviser for advice on which investment trust will meet your needs.

'I'm already seeing a sizeable **profit**'

When in his early 30s, Dominic Little, 38, was near the peak of his earning capacity and unburdened by the high costs of a growing family. Finding himself in this position, he decided he wanted to do something with his money.

'I was looking through my bank statements one month and was horrified at just how much money I was wasting,' says Dominic, an IT manager. 'I was spending far too much on going out and was hardly saving any money at all.'

Dominic did have some savings in a building society but they were not earning very much. 'I wanted to make sure the extra money I planned to save would earn much more,' he says. 'The only snag was, I didn't know how to invest in shares or which ones to buy. So I read through the money pages in a newspaper one weekend and saw that unit trusts and investment trusts did quite well.

'I only put £50 a month into my unit trust and I'm already seeing a sizeable profit. It's easy, I don't miss the cash and I don't need to be a share expert as the fund manager does all the hard work for me.'

As with all shares, there is a difference between the buying and selling price of the share (see page 44). In addition, investment trust shares can trade at a discount or premium — they are worth either less or more than the underlying investments they hold. This depends on supply and demand for the shares. If, for example, the investment trust is out of favour, the total value of its shares can be worth less than all the investments it owns. If the discount narrows, however, investors can make a profit even if the underlying investments have not increased in value.

How are investment trust shares priced?

Investment trusts are taxed in the same way as any share (see page 48) – you pay capital gains tax on your profit above a certain level and tax is deducted from your dividend income.

How will I be taxed?

For more information, contact the Association of Investment Trust Companies (AITC) on 020 7282 5555.

How do I find out more?

---

choosing an investment

How do unit trusts, investment trusts and OEICs compare? In general there is little difference between a unit trust and an OEIC (see page 57), although OEICs may be easier to understand because their shares have only a single price.

There is more of a difference between investment trusts and unit trusts. Historically, the best-performing investment trusts have produced higher returns than the best unit trusts. However, the worst-performing investment trusts have lost far more than the worst unit trusts.

Investment trusts are more volatile than unit trusts – they have bigger rises and falls in prices – and their complex structure can make them more difficult to understand than unit trusts.

If you're ignoring the opportunities for
tax-free investing, you might as well be
throwing your money down the drain

Tax-free investing

Most people can escape paying tax on the profits they make from investments, yet only a fraction of the money in the stock market is invested via tax-free schemes.

If you are one of those investors who's paying tax needlessly, it may be because you are unaware of the tax-free schemes on offer and just how easy it is to invest in them.

This year you are entitled to invest up to £7,000 in the stock market tax free through an Individual Savings Account (ISA) (from April 2001 this drops to £5,000) and up to £270 in a friendly society tax-exempt scheme. In addition, pay-outs from life insurance investments, such as with-profits bonds, are usually tax free. If you've invested money in Personal Equity Plans (PEPs), these can continue to grow tax free, too.

You can start investing in a tax-free scheme with just £20, and you can have instant access to your cash if you have to get your hands on it in a hurry. You don't have to pay extra to invest in a tax-free scheme (in fact, some of them are the cheapest forms of stock market investment) and you don't have to declare your profits on your tax return.

Stocks and shares ISAs

What is a stocks and shares ISA?

A stocks and shares ISA is one element of the tax-free savings scheme introduced by the government in April 1999. The scheme allows you to invest up to a certain amount in individual shares, unit trusts, investment trusts and OEICs, and fixed-interest investments, such as bonds and gilts, without paying income or capital gains tax on the money you make. These share-based investments can be held in either a mini ISA or a maxi ISA. For information on the limits and rules applying to the different types of ISA, see page 30.

Is a stocks and shares ISA right for me?

If you are prepared to take an element of risk with your money in exchange for the possibility of earning more than you would with a savings account, and are prepared to tie up your cash for at least a couple of years, the answer is yes.

Which is best: mini ISAs or a maxi ISA?

This depends on what else you want to invest in and how much you want to invest in stocks and shares.

If you want to maximise the total you can invest in stocks and shares tax free, a maxi ISA is the best choice. It allows you to invest up to £7,000 in the stock market in this tax year and up to £5,000 from 6 April 2001. If you want to save some cash tax free as well, a maxi ISA allows you to invest up to £4,000 in stocks and shares and up to £3,000 in cash savings.

If you opt for mini ISAs, you will only be able to invest up to £3,000 in stocks and shares and £3,000 in savings – giving you only £6,000 in tax-free investments and savings. Only if you want to put money into all three different types of ISA investment – cash, stocks and shares, and life insurance investments – should you consider mini ISAs.

The drawback of a maxi ISA is that all the investments must be managed by one company – so you need to pick a company that offers both good savings rates and attractive stocks and shares products. With a mini ISA you can use a different management company for each type of investment.

An ISA is not an investment in itself – it is a tax-free wrapper that can be put around an investment. So, instead of buying a unit trust, you ask to buy a unit trust ISA. There is no difference between the two, other than that the profits on the investment held in the ISA are tax free.

How do I buy a stocks and shares ISA?

You have to buy your ISA from an approved provider. For a stocks and shares mini ISA or a maxi ISA, this can include a unit trust fund management company, a stockbroker or even a supermarket. If you want advice on which ISA to buy, you can buy through an independent financial adviser.

Forget the fact that your investment is in an ISA. Select it because it's a good investment, not because it's tax free.

How do I pick an ISA?

An ISA is like a tax-free wrapping that you can put around your savings and investments

Does an ISA cost more? An ISA doesn't usually cost any more than other types of investment. Investment trusts can charge more to invest via an ISA if you buy directly from them, rather than through a stockbroker, but in most cases the charges are the same as for their regular savings schemes and are very low. A few companies, however, charge a set fee rather than a percentage of the amount invested. This can be as much as £50 as an initial charge and £60 as an annual charge, which will eat into your capital, particularly if you are not investing the maximum.

Unit trust ISAs cost exactly the same as unit trusts. In fact, competition among fund managers and the new CAT standards mean that, in some cases, the cost of investing in a unit trust has come down.

Individual share ISAs tend to be more expensive – but this reflects the fact that buying individual shares tends to cost more than buying a collective investment. If you buy an individual share ISA, you will usually pay a dealing charge as well as an administration fee of around 0.6% a year.

> ### your **decision**
>
> If you buy a unit trust ISA through a discount broker, some of the initial charge will be refunded to you. However, if you take this route, rather than buying through an independent financial adviser, you will get no advice on whether the product you choose is best for you.

Is it worth going for a CAT-marked fund? CAT stands for low Charges, easy Access and fair Terms. To qualify for a CAT mark, a stocks and shares ISA must have:
- Only one charge – an annual fee of no more than 1% of what is invested. There should be no additional initial charge.
- A minimum investment limit set no higher than £50 a month or £500 a year.

Funds with low charges are not necessarily
the best deal. Sometimes, paying more will get
you access to the very best performers

Opinion is split over whether CAT funds offer the best deal.
Supporters of the CAT standard say that lower charges mean
investors see a better return on their money. Those who have
not adopted the CAT standard claim that it can be worth
paying more charges if it means investment funds are better
managed and therefore perform better.

When you choose an ISA, charges should be just one of the
factors you consider. An investment's performance track
record should be your priority.

Even non-taxpayers should consider an ISA. You may
become a taxpayer later on or, if your investments do well,
you could find that you become liable to capital gains tax.

**I don't pay tax
– should I still
buy an ISA?**

'Our ISA **mortgage** is totally **flexible**'

Like many homebuyers, Vik and Nimisha Patel want to pay off their mortgage as quickly as possible. However, instead of paying extra to their mortgage lender each month, they are investing their cash in an ISA.

'A few years ago we would have been advised to take out an endowment policy,' says Nimisha, a mum of two with a part-time job in customer services. 'But you will know about all the bad publicity surrounding them. What we've got is a far more flexible investment and, hopefully, one that'll produce a bigger lump sum in the end.

'We have an interest-only mortgage, which means we pay only the interest on it each month – this is cheaper than a repayment loan. And then we invest £150 a month in our ISA. Although we pay more than we strictly have to, we hope that our money will grow quickly – and tax free – so we can pay off the mortgage after 15 or 18 years, rather than 25.

'The other advantage of the ISA is that it's totally flexible. If we want, we can change our monthly payments or cash it in to pay off the mortgage. And if we want to switch mortgages, we can keep our ISA going rather than take out another investment.'

The Patels' ISA cash is invested in two unit trust ISAs – one is a tracker fund, which should match the growth of the stock market, and one is a UK general fund from a top fund manager.

'As we're investing for the longer term, we could have opted for something a little more risky, but we decided to play safe,' says Nimisha. 'After all, our home is at stake.'

Personal Equity Plans (PEPs)

PEP stands for Personal Equity Plan. These were withdrawn from sale in April 1999 and replaced by ISAs.

What is a PEP?

No. You would have to sell your PEP and then reinvest some of the proceeds in an ISA. Selling your PEP means you would lose your PEP tax break for ever. What's more, you were allowed to invest far more in a PEP (£6,000 in a main PEP and £3,000 in a single company PEP) than you can in an ISA. By keeping your PEP running and opening an ISA too, you can maximise the amount you can invest tax free.

Can I switch my PEP to an ISA?

You should monitor the performance of your PEP to check it's still producing the best return. If you're unhappy with the performance of your PEP, you can either switch it to another fund run by the same PEP manager (this can often be done quite cheaply) or switch it to a fund run by a different manager (this means you'll incur a fresh set of initial charges).

PEPs are very similar to stocks and shares ISAs – tax-free wrappers around investments. As far more is invested in PEPs than ISAs – PEPs were running for a decade and attracted £70 billion of investors' money – it is vital you don't forget about any money you have tied up in a PEP.

What should I do with my PEP?

Most PEP holders chose to put their investments into UK funds. If you were one of them, you may want to consider using your stocks and shares mini ISA or your maxi ISA to diversify into overseas markets, such as Europe or the USA.

If I have a PEP, which ISA should I buy?

Life insurance ISAs

What is a life
insurance ISA?

A life insurance ISA is one element of the tax-free savings scheme introduced by the government in April 1999. Each tax year you are allowed to invest up to £1,000 tax free in life insurance investments, either through a mini ISA or as part of a maxi ISA (see page 30). Life insurance investments are investment plans run by life insurance companies. They should not be confused with life insurance policies.

What type of
investment
do I get?

The most common product is a with-profits bond. This is an investment bond that invests in a broad mix of shares, property, bonds, gilts and cash. With-profits bonds are designed to smooth out the ups and downs of investment performance by paying an annual bonus. In addition, investors may earn a final bonus when the policy matures – this represents the investor's share in the growth of the fund.

The with-profits
bonds offered by life
insurance companies
are designed to iron
out the rises and
falls of investment
performance

Some life insurance investments can produce solid returns (although probably not as high as stocks and shares) and have the advantage of being relatively low risk.

Is a life insurance ISA right for me?

With-profits bonds (see opposite) are popular with older savers as they can pay a regular income. In theory you can get your cash back at any time, but you generally need to invest for at least five years to make this type of investment worth while – you're only guaranteed to get the value of your premiums back after three years of investing. Beware of bonds that include a 'market value adjuster' – this allows the insurance company to cut the size of your fund if you sell during a period of bad performance.

Charges for life insurance investments tend to be high – the CAT standard for life insurance ISAs rules that the annual fee must be no more than 3% of the total fund (compared with 1% for a stocks and shares ISA). To qualify for a CAT mark a life insurance ISA must also have a minimum premium of no more than £25 a month or £250 a year.

How much does a life insurance ISA cost?

friendly societies

Friendly societies are similar to mutual building societies in that they are owned by their members. However, rather than taking deposits and offering mortgages, they sell life insurance investments. These include tax-exempt policies.

You can invest up to £270 a year as a lump sum or up to £25 a month in regular savings in a friendly society tax-exempt policy. Generally you need to keep this type of policy going for 10 years to get a decent return. If you cash in your policy before this, you may not even get back your original investment.

Jargon buster

AER Annual Equivalent Rate – the interest you would earn in a year if you left all your monthly interest in your savings account

All Share Index All companies listed on the UK stock market

Alternative Investment Market (AIM) An index of companies hoping to get a full listing on the main stock market

Annual management charge A charge, usually a percentage of the value of your investment, deducted from your investment each year

APS scheme Approved Profit Sharing scheme – gives employees a share in their company's profits in the form of free shares

Base rate Interest rate set by the Bank of England, used to determine borrowing and savings rates

Bid-offer spread The difference between the buying (offer) price and selling (bid) price of a share

Bid price The price at which you can sell shares or units back to a company or investment manager

Blue-chip stocks Shares in large companies, usually household names and in the FTSE 100

Bond Issued by companies to raise finance. Bonds pay interest to their holders, rather than dividends

Bond fund A type of unit trust investing in bonds, rather than shares, and paying investors an income

Bonus account A savings account that pays a bonus if you keep your money invested for a set period

Capital Your original investment

Capital gains tax A tax on the increase in the value of an asset, such as a share, since you bought it

Capital share A share in an investment trust for investors who want to see their capital grow

Cash ISA An account that allows you to earn interest tax free on cash savings

CAT standard A voluntary standard, set by the government, covering Charges, Access and Terms for ISAs

Certificated share A share for which you receive a share certificate and which gives you the right to vote at annual general meetings

Collective investments The money of many investors collected together by an investment manager and invested in the stock market

Crest The settlement system for UK shares. The shares are traded in electronic form

Discount broker A person who sells unit trusts and rebates some of the initial charge back to the investor

Dividend Money paid to shareholders representing their share of the company's profits over a certain period

Employee share scheme A scheme that allows employees to buy shares, often at a discount, in the company they work for

Flotation When a company joins the stock market and starts to sell its shares

Footsie Another name for the FTSE 100 Index

Friendly society An organisation that sells tax-exempt life insurance investments

FTSE 100 Index An index of the 100 largest companies by value whose shares are traded on the UK stock market

FTSE 250 Index The 250 largest UK companies by share value

Fund manager The expert who decides how money in a unit or investment trust should be invested

Gilt A type of bond issued by the government that pays interest over a set term

Gross interest The interest you earn on your savings before income tax is deducted

High-interest cheque account An account that pays a rate similar to a savings account but also offers a cheque-book facility

Income share A share in an investment trust for investors who want to earn an income

Index-linked Certificates A form of National Savings in which the rate of interest is fixed at a certain level above the rate of inflation

Initial charge A one-off charge deducted from your capital when you first invest in a unit trust

Instant-access account A savings account that allows you to withdraw money whenever you want to without penalty

Interest-bearing current account A bank or building society account offering a cheque book and cash card, and paying interest on the account balance

Investment trust A listed company that invests in other companies around the world, and sells its own shares to investors

ISA Individual Savings Account – a tax-free savings scheme introduced by the government in April 1999

Life insurance ISA An ISA that allows you to invest in life insurance investments without paying tax on the money you make

Maxi ISA A tax-free savings account in which you can invest up to £7,000 tax free. You can invest either the full amount in stocks and shares or up to £3,000 in cash savings and up to £1,000 in life insurance investments

Mid price The price of shares as quoted in newspapers, midway between the bid and offer prices

Mini ISA A tax-free savings account that allows you to invest in cash savings, stocks and shares or life insurance investments. You can have one of each type of mini Isa in each tax year

National Savings Tax-free savings accounts run by the government

Net interest The interest you earn on your savings after tax at basic rate has been deducted

Nominee share A share with no share certificate, held in a nominee account by a broker

Notice account A savings account that requires you to give 30, 60, 75 or 90 days' notice before you withdraw your money

OEIC A unit trust that has converted into a company

Offer price The price at which you can buy shares or units from a company or investment manager

Offshore savings Savings accounts held in places such as the Isle of Man, Guernsey or Jersey

Personal Equity Plan (PEP)
A form of tax-free investment,
withdrawn from sale in April 1999

Quoted company Any company
that is trading on the stock market

Savings bond A savings account
that ties up your cash for a set
period but pays a comparatively
high rate of interest

Savings Certificates A form of
National Savings that pay a fixed
rate of interest over a set term

SAYE scheme Allows employees
to save for the purchase of shares
in the company they work for

Share A legal document that gives
its holder part ownership of the
company that issues the share

Share club A group of people who
pool cash to buy shares

Share option scheme A scheme
giving an employee the right to buy
shares in the company in future but
at the present price

Shareholder perk An incentive
given to shareholders by
companies to promote loyalty

Stock market Where shares and
equities are bought and sold

Stockbroker Someone who
advises on which shares to buy
and buys them on your behalf

Stocks and shares ISA An ISA
that allows you to invest in stocks
and shares without paying tax on
the money you make

**TESSA (Tax-Exempt Special
Savings Account)** A form of tax-
free saving, withdrawn in April 1999

TESSA-only ISA A savings account
that provides a tax-free home for
capital from a mature TESSA

Tiered rate An interest rate that
varies depending on how much is
deposited in a savings account

Tracker account A savings account
with an interest rate that tracks
changes in general interest rates

Tracker fund A type of unit trust
that tracks a stock market index
such as the FTSE 100

Unit trust An investment fund, split
into units of equal value, which
investors can buy

With-profits bond An investment
plan that awards an annual bonus
to investors, who may also choose
to take a regular income

Index